Daybreakers

CLIFFORD WILLIAMS

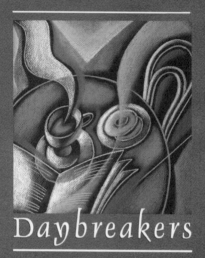

Daybreakers

365 EYE-OPENING REFLECTIONS

 SORIN BOOKS   Notre Dame, IN

www.sorinbooks.com

International Standard Book Number: 1-893732-52-5

Cover by Eric Walljasper

Text design by Kathy Robinson Coleman

Printed and bound in the United States of America.

Library of Congress Cataloging-in-Publication Data

Williams, Clifford, 1943-
Daybreakers : 365 eye-opening reflections / Clifford
Williams.
  p. cm.
ISBN 1-893732-52-5
  1. Spiritual life--Christianity. 2. Devotional calendars. I.
Title.
BV4501.3 .W545 2002
242'.2--dc21

                                          2002003133
                                                CIP

Contents

Introduction

We are deeply divided. Although we are often loving and compassionate, we are also incurably self-centered. We feel both pleasure and shame when we catch ourselves being greedy or envious. We pursue eternal values yet indulge in the trivialities of this world.

This dividedness especially affects those of us who are religious or who have spiritual aims. We have a heightened desire to root out apathy and excess anger. At the same time, these rumble around inside us, often without our being aware of them.

What we want, at bottom, is to be free from this inner conflict, for it is a torment to the sensitive soul. We desire what I call "singleness of heart." This is the pursuit of the good without ulterior or conflicting aims. It is present when our motives are pure and simple, when we are not pulled in different directions.

Daybreakers contains 365 aphorisms on the search for singleness of heart, divided into 52 sections, one for each week of the year. Each section begins with two or three short paragraphs introducing the motif of that week's aphorisms. The book as a whole has a "problem-solution" progression. The first two quarters focus on inner spiritual conflict, and the second two quarters focus on ways to move beyond it.

The first two quarters contain the bad news—things are worse than we imagine. They are also far better, and the second two quarters explain how this is so. Remaining in the bad news will produce a bitter taste, but moving beyond it to the good news will produce sweetness and hope.

The aphorisms are designed to be accessible on first reading yet to invite further reflection. One can return to them and gain fresh insights. It is often what aphorisms do not say that gives them their significance, and pausing to consider the unsaid is likely to produce more insight than a quick reading.

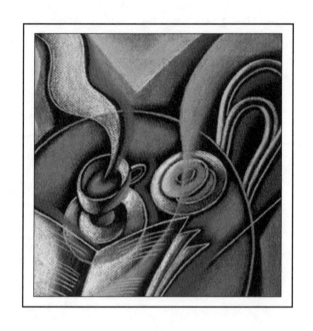

First Quarter

Where Are We Headed?

Travelers must know where they are going if they expect to get to a definite place. They cannot just set out aimlessly and hope to arrive at their destination. If they do not know where they are and where they want to go, they will wander haphazardly, lost and bewildered. Or, what is worse, they will give up and make no effort to go any particular place, perhaps even forgetting that they are lost.

It is the same for our journey to eternity. We must have some notion of where we want to go and what our current condition is. The weeks in this first quarter focus on discovering both our aim and our condition. We are not ordinarily conscious of these, but it is imperative that we become so. Otherwise we may be like the traveler who simply wanders.

Week I

Pursuing the Eternal

The real business of life is the pursuit of eternity. We do not, of course, constantly have eternity on our minds. In fact, very few of our conscious thoughts focus on it. Yet we definitely engage in the pursuit. When we gaze at the stars, we are looking for something larger than ourselves. When we touch a despairing friend, we are setting aside our own cares. As we sit quietly observing passing people, we are searching for knowledge of our own inner selves. Our scrambles for attention are ways of making our lives count.

These facts show that what we want from life is the sense that a day's activities have a larger significance. We desire for them to possess a meaning that will be worth something when we die. This is the essence of our pursuit of eternity.

☀ Sunday

If we cannot say we have lived well, then nothing else matters.

☀ Monday

The dread of insignificance motivates even our idle conversations.

☀ Tuesday

We work hard to get ahead, but rarely ask what the point of getting ahead is.

☀ Wednesday

The surest way to get a knot in the bottom of our stomachs is to come to believe that we have wasted our lives.

☀ Thursday

We may know what we want from an afternoon of play, but may not know what we want from life.

☀ Friday

Our intense desire for significance makes us turn our least activities into monuments to ourselves.

☀ Saturday

Most people have no idea what the driving force of their lives is—they simply let themselves be driven.

Week 2

Discovering Our Deepest Desires

We know what most of our everyday desires are—they lie on the surface of our consciousness. Rarely, though, are we aware of our rock-bottom desires, the ones dealing with our lives as a whole. They usually lie below the surface of normal awareness. Only sporadically do they pop up to the surface, and then only for fleeting seconds.

If we could uncover these basic desires, we would know what we hope to get out of life. And if we could stay conscious of them, we might be drawn to them more.

The trick, though, is to become aware of them. It is not impossible, but it is often difficult.

☀ Sunday

The truest way to discover what we value is to look at what we do.

☀ Monday

Without numerous pauses in life's mad rush, we are liable not to know where we are heading.

☀ Tuesday

The real drama of life involves our sorrows and delights, anticipations and regrets, sighings and dreads.

☀ Wednesday

We could discover our rock bottom drives if we could get behind the pulsating mass of thoughts that normally inhabits our conscious life.

☀ Thursday

The deepest desires of the human heart are rarely expressed in words.

☀ Friday

What we devote our emotional energy to is a clue to what concerns us most.

☀ Saturday

If we could catch our passing daydreams, we could ascertain what we really love.

Week 3

Intimations of Eternity

Sometimes the eternal breaks through to us sharply and vividly. Most of the time, though, it comes gently and obscured. These latter occasions are more like hints than open declarations. They are inklings of something larger, clues that life is more than what we can hold in our hands.

Many of these intimations of eternity occur as we go about our everyday tasks. We may be on our way to work and glimpse new ways we can love our family members. Or we may be in the midst of housework and suddenly wonder what we will be like when we are old.

If we are not alert, we will let these occasions slip by with little thought. What we need to do is to listen to them, for they reveal our true calling.

✪ Sunday

Our sense of unfulfilled love is a longing for eternity, though we rarely recognize it as that.

✪ Monday

Caring not for trivial pursuits indicates a heart set on significance.

✪ Tuesday

The truest stance toward eternity is to feel homesick for it.

✪ Wednesday

Desire for an undisturbed heart is a sign of yearning for the eternal.

✪ Thursday

To perceive that something is missing from our daily routines is to discern a call from eternity.

✪ Friday

The faraway look in our eyes as we sit thinking about life springs from our desire for what is eternal.

✪ Saturday

Sensing the tragedy and beauty in our lives heightens our craving for eternity.

Week 4

Yearning for Something More

What defines the human heart is its yearnings. These are the cravings that often go unnamed, the aches that haunt us from time to time. They involve the sense that something is missing from our lives plus the unsettled desire to possess that something.

Sometimes these yearnings are fairly specific: they may be for a lifelong companion or for release from a painful memory. Other times they are vague and indefinite: we are not too sure what would satisfy them, though we do know that we are dissatisfied with the way things are.

The one thing we must not do is to ignore these deep yearnings. That is one of our biggest temptations—to immerse ourselves so much in daily duties that we do not listen to what our hearts are telling us.

✸ Sunday

The mark of a spiritual searcher is to be
continually looking for the "something more"
that is missing from one's life.

✸ Monday

Our moments of cosmic wistfulness, though faint,
reveal the truest desires of our heart.

✸ Tuesday

Our longing for authentic love often remains
merely a longing.

✸ Wednesday

We are—most of us—desperate souls searching
for release from acute inner conflict.

✸ Thursday

One of our strongest cravings is to count for something, but seldom are we sure how to satisfy it.

✸ Friday

We would shrivel up if ever a sense of
insignificance consumed us.

✸ Saturday

Our desire for an uncluttered heart is undermined
by a thousand distractions.

Week 5

Restlessness

When we are restless, we cast about for something different to do. We are unsettled and fidgety. Perhaps obtaining some new friend, or going someplace we haven't been, or buying something would make a difference, we think. To stifle our unease, we plan a project or turn on the television.

These reactions show that our first instinct is to squash our moments of restlessness. We want to escape the sense of emptiness that comes upon us.

If, however, we paused and listened to our restless yearnings, we might look for meaning more energetically. We might discover that we need to change our preferences. And we might even find that it is only the eternal that can fill our hollowness permanently.

☀ Sunday

Whole-life restlessness is motivated by the unrecognized desire to give ourselves to something divine.

☀ Monday

A restless mind makes quiet meditation rare.

☀ Tuesday

We use adventure and excitement as antidotes to boredom and drudgery, little realizing that they can be just as empty.

☀ Wednesday

When everything seems hollow, we gaze at life with a vacant stare.

☀ Thursday

The busyness of everyday living is occasionally punctured by little stabs of restlessness.

☀ Friday

Craving eternity is like aching to be with a beloved: we are restless and discontent without the object of our passion.

☀ Saturday

Our restless sighings are yearnings for unspoiled love.

Week 6

Looking for Meaning

We possess mixed sentiments about meaning. On the one hand, we want our activities and projects to possess meaning. If they result in something worthwhile, we feel satisfied. If they do not, we feel as if our time spent on them has been wasted. The same is true of our lives as a whole. We want them to have a point as well. This desire is so strong that we could not live if we thought they had no significance.

On the other hand, we suppress this drive for meaning. We do so by immersing ourselves in what we are doing—our jobs, hobbies, and entertainment. Our absorption in these activities causes the question of what we are living for to fade. We do not want to think about it, afraid perhaps that we will discover that we have no ultimate meaning.

What we must do is activate the first sentiment and deactivate the second. We will not find meaning if we constantly suppress our drive for it.

✴ Sunday

It is much more than simple aversion we have toward feeling that our lives do not count for anything; it is desperate dread.

✴ Monday

Cosmic indifference is not caring whether we waste our whole lives.

✴ Tuesday

A few hours of mind-numbing activity is often a welcome escape; a whole life of mind-numbing activity is a tragic escape.

✴ Wednesday

Though we think that diversion from dull routine is an antidote to boredom, it can be as pointless as dull routine.

✴ Thursday

Most of us drift through life giving little thought to where we are going.

✴ Friday

The true tragedies of life take place inside us—and so does the true beauty.

✴ Saturday

If we thoughtlessly let our inclinations and pleasures take us wherever they will, then meaning does not matter much to us.

Week 7

Wasting Life

"That was a waste," we sometimes say after doing something which did not turn out as we wished. It bothers us when this happens, but we soon get over it and move on to something else. We would not get over it so easily, however, if we felt that our whole lives had been wasted. We would be very uneasy and would be tempted to set the feeling aside without dealing with it. That, in fact, is what we often do. In a quiet moment, the thought that much of what we do is trivial pops into our mind, but we quickly let other thoughts crowd it out. Or we may busy ourselves in some activity so as to avoid pursuing the matter.

We need to pursue the matter, though, for if we do not, we may end up actually wasting our lives. That would be the ultimate tragedy.

✦ Sunday

There is only one question we need
to answer—"Am I squandering my life?"

✦ Monday

The most difficult part of taking inventory of our
lives is overcoming the fear of doing so.

✦ Tuesday

Little produces more distress at the end of one's
life than the sense of having wasted it.

✦ Wednesday

If we were more conscious of our craving for
significance, we would give up many of the
pointless and trivial ways we try to satisfy it.

✦ Thursday

Some people live as if they are acting in a play.
When the play is done, God will say, "Good
acting, but you missed the point."

✦ Friday

The trouble with building an edifice of
self-glorifying accomplishments is that it
crumbles when we die.

✦ Saturday

If we do not ask ourselves now what we will
think of our lives from the vantage point of old
age, we probably will not ask then either.

Week 8

The Hidden Self

One of the most disturbing facts about our motives is that some of them are hidden, so that what we do sometimes springs from unrecognized motives. For example, some of what we do is a result of the unacknowledged desire to be admired—we want to be noticed for our virtue, we like to think of ourselves as better than others, and we like to congratulate ourselves when we have done something especially good.

Sometimes we see these motives clearly, but often we do not. It is as if they are in the peripheral parts of our vision or obscured entirely from our sight. In order to root them out, we need to become fully aware of them. Otherwise, they will control us.

✺ Sunday

To encounter our hidden motives is to lose our innocence.

✺ Monday

The discovery that we have been hiding from God when we comfortably thought we were seeking God is as startling as it is unsettling.

✺ Tuesday

The enemy within is usually in hiding.

✺ Wednesday

If we dared admit to ourselves all of our ulterior motives, we would instinctively recoil from them.

✺ Thursday

Our hidden selves frequently want to stay hidden.

✺ Friday

We may think we have rid ourselves of some unsavory motive, but it returns in ways almost too subtle to detect.

✺ Saturday

We know a good deal less of ourselves than we want to admit.

Week 9

Secrets

Fyodor Dostoyevsky, the Russian novelist, once wrote, "There are certain things in a man's past which he does not divulge to everybody but, perhaps, only to his friends. Again there are certain things he will not divulge even to his friends; he will divulge them perhaps only to himself, and that, too, as a secret. But, finally, there are things which he is afraid to divulge even to himself, and every decent man has quite an accumulation of such things in his mind."

What Dostoyevsky says is surely true—we all have secrets. Some of them we can share with close friends, but others we do not want to tell anyone. Some secrets, in fact, we keep even from ourselves. These are often the most dangerous ones to have.

✺ Sunday

The secrets we are afraid to uncover in ourselves
are the ones we most need to know.

✺ Monday

We secretly want recognition for our
virtues—all of them.

✺ Tuesday

Though we detest it in others and recoil from it in
ourselves, we secretly like to put on a good front.

✺ Wednesday

Our greatest fear is to have our secrets discovered
by others.

✺ Thursday

If we are afraid to divulge a secret about
ourselves, it is because doing so would
produce severe shame or guilt.

✺ Friday

One of the secrets we do not want to admit is
that we crave to be thought of as a great person,
admired and revered by all.

✺ Saturday

The secrets we keep from ourselves are the ones
we relish most.

Week 10

Self-Watching

When Socrates declared that the unexamined life is not worth living, he meant to goad his listeners into becoming self-watchers. Being one, he thought, is a sign that one cares for one's soul.

If this is true, and if we care about meaning and whole-life goals, we will become alert to what is going on in the deep recesses of our souls. For it is there that our ultimate direction is determined.

At the same time, we will take care not to be consumed by self-watching, for too much of it can be debilitating. It is better not to probe our inner selves if doing so makes us unable to focus on what is good, but it is better still to scrutinize and examine with the aim of becoming good.

☀ Sunday

We do not need special training to become a
self-watcher, but we do need to train
ourselves to become one.

☀ Monday

Too much self-interrogation may make us morose;
too little may make us superficial.

☀ Tuesday

The mark of an active self-investigator is to be
discontent with mere appearances of oneself.

☀ Wednesday

We cannot gaze for long at our
own moral failings.

☀ Thursday

Restoring a childlike faith requires a
self-examination which, if wallowed in,
would undermine the faith.

☀ Friday

We like speculating about ulterior motives in
others, but dislike investigating them in ourselves.

☀ Saturday

Intense self-watching may produce more
self-centeredness than self-knowledge.

Week 11

Spiritual Ambivalence

We are ambivalent toward someone when we are both attracted to them and repelled by them. Perhaps they have an engaging smile, but a grating manner of speaking. Or perhaps they are gracious to us sometimes but unkind other times. We are, as a consequence, pulled in different directions—we like to be with them but try to steer clear of them as well.

This same phenomenon occurs in our moral and spiritual lives. Though we genuinely want to be loving, kind, and generous, we also want not to be. We want to be outgoing in the way these require, but at the same time want to be absorbed with our own concerns. We want to be courteous to someone who has hurt us yet desire to retaliate for the injury done to us.

Knowing our true selves requires that we acknowledge our ambivalences.

☀ Sunday

We both seek and resist knowledge of our
deepest motives.

☀ Monday

Though we are uncomfortable when someone
congratulates us, we also delight in it.

☀ Tuesday

We are charmed by the thought that we are better
than everyone else, but shamed when we catch
ourselves having it.

☀ Wednesday

The desire to use others to enhance our sense of
self-importance often resides side by side with
genuine respect for them.

☀ Thursday

We want to give love without reserve, but are
fearful of doing so.

☀ Friday

The most maddening form of dividedness occurs
when we are acutely conscious of it.

☀ Saturday

Although we desire to be genuinely virtuous,
we sometimes would rather just appear
to be virtuous.

Week 12

A Tangled Mass

Augustine once anguished, "Who can untie this most twisted and intricate mass of knots?" He was referring to his attempt to disentangle the complex jumble of desires in him. He saw all too clearly the way in which these desires held him in their iron grip. He recognized that behind one motive there might lie another, that excising one desire might involve excising another. He perceived that desires come in various degrees and that we are moved first by one then another, apparently randomly. The more Augustine probed, the more he knew, but also the more baffled he became.

When we become self-watchers, we certainly come to know more about ourselves. At the same time, we realize that we possess depths we may never get to the bottom of and complexity we may never unravel. This is cause for frustration and agony on the one hand, and wonder and amazement on the other.

☀ Sunday

It is possible to have both genuine and ulterior motives, but it is often hard to disentangle them from each other.

☀ Monday

The trouble with unconscious motives is that they are unconscious.

☀ Tuesday

There are very few deliberate hypocrites.

☀ Wednesday

Some of our desires are plain and apparent and some are buried beneath mounds of other desires.

☀ Thursday

We would become instantly terrified if acquaintances could suddenly peer into our inner lives.

☀ Friday

An exalted sense of our importance seeps into nearly every thought about ourselves.

☀ Saturday

We are quick to spot another's weaknesses, but rarely notice them in ourselves.

Week 13

Strangers to Ourselves

If some of our motives and desires are hidden from us, or even half-hidden, then we know ourselves less than we think we do. We may know our everyday likes, to be sure, but if we do not know our root motives, the ones that really drive us, then at a basic level we are strangers to ourselves. This is a most unsettling realization.

We need not be distressed at this realization, though, for the truth is that we are mixtures of self-ignorance and self-knowledge. Though we are not entirely transparent to ourselves, we are not entirely strangers to ourselves, either. As we pursue the eternal, we become less and less strangers and more and more transparent to ourselves.

✦ Sunday

If we want to know whether we are what we appear to be, we need to poke around in our inner selves.

✦ Monday

We sometimes mistakenly regard a general truth about humankind as a deep truth about ourselves.

✦ Tuesday

Pretending to ourselves to be different from what we actually are is like pretending to others to be cheerier than we really are.

✦ Wednesday

If we live on borrowed beliefs, we are not who we think we are.

✦ Thursday

To be honest with ourselves, we must be willing to unmask our illusions.

✦ Friday

In some ways we know less about ourselves than do cursory acquaintances.

✦ Saturday

When we regard ourselves simply as an object of curiosity, we deftly evade real self-knowledge.

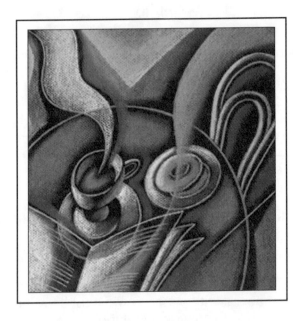

Second Quarter

Obstacles
Along the Way

Paul Revere once declared that eternal vigilance is the price of liberty. The same is true of our journey to eternity. It requires constant vigilance against numerous obstacles. Not only must we be aware of these obstacles, we have to battle them continually. If we are not on our guard, they will assail us, often without our being aware of their doing so.

Imagination, for example, sometimes leads us to be more satisfied with imaginary love than with real love. Constant motion distracts us from what really counts—we hurry here and there without asking why. Indifference casts a pall over our entire spiritual life—we shrug our shoulders about cosmic matters. And outright resistance—the "Stay away from me" disposition that we take toward goodness—infects our basic stance toward the eternal.

In this quarter we will look at a number of obstacles to pursuing eternity. They are largely inner desires, passions, and urges, most of which go unnoticed by us. This means that they can do their jobs easily and often. When we cast a piercing light on them, however, they begin to lose their power over us. The more we can subject these obstacles to our penetrating gaze, the better.

Week 14

Wanting to Be
Better Than Others

One of our most intractable "needs" is to feel that we are better than others in some respect. If an acquaintance wins an award, we immediately think of an accomplishment that distinguishes us. When someone fails, we congratulate ourselves on being successful. Public praise for another elicits the thought that we, too, deserve praise. We could not live for long if we did not believe that our talents and qualities are superior in some way to those of at least some other people. Or so we think.

The truth is that we can get along quite well without needing to feel better than others. With a solid sense of self-worth, we will not need to feed a starving ego. Most of us, however, wrestle with self-worth. Thoughts of superiority constantly arise in our minds. Sometimes they are clear and prominent, and other times they are subtle and devious. Our aim should be to notice them and then to refrain from nurturing them.

✸ Sunday

The chief satisfaction in being good sometimes lies in knowing that someone else is not as good.

✸ Monday

Who of us does not like to conceive of ourselves as different from the general run of humanity?

✸ Tuesday

Pride in having done well easily slips into pride in having done better than others.

✸ Wednesday

If our jobs give us a sense of mission, we are tempted to distinguish ourselves from those whose jobs we believe are not as significant.

✸ Thursday

One of our most gratifying thoughts is to imagine ourselves the best there is.

✸ Friday

Being religious may tempt one to think, "I am better than people who are not religious."

✸ Saturday

If we regard ourselves as superior to others, it will eventually come through in what we say.

Week 15

Looking for Admiration

We want not only to feel better than others, but actually to be better. When we are better, we know we will be admired. We strive to do well in our jobs so that our co-workers will esteem us. We buy clothes that we think will cause our acquaintances to admire us. We invest a great deal of energy in our projects so that those who observe the results will regard us highly.

It is not too strong to say that our desire for admiration is a craving, almost a lust. If we did not get a daily dose, we would feel greatly diminished. So we pursue it in countless ways. We use even the most innocent of actions to secure it. What we do may appear to others to be purely motivated, but in reality we often hope to be admired for it.

☀ Sunday

If our energy level increases when we know we are being watched, we are probably driven by a desire for admiration.

☀ Monday

The smallest bit of public recognition sparks in us a wild desire for more.

☀ Tuesday

We delight in giving words of encouragement—and in being admired for doing so.

☀ Wednesday

The thought of being admired for our compassion is sometimes a stronger motivator than the goodness of the compassion.

☀ Thursday

If we like being esteemed for our religious goodness, we are more of a Pharisee than we suspect.

☀ Friday

Virtue is its own reward—when we do not use it to obtain admiration.

☀ Saturday

Images of ourselves being loving easily turn into images of others admiring us for being loving.

Week 16

Admiring Ourselves

Not only do we like it when others admire us, we also like to admire ourselves. The first, in fact, feeds the second. When someone congratulates us on a job well done, we are prone to congratulate ourselves. If we know that we are respected for our virtues, we are likely to compliment ourselves as a result.

The trouble with admiring ourselves is that it tends to become excessive. Our sense of worth expands so much that we begin to feel that we are quite exceptional persons. We feel special and unique (which, of course, everyone is), so much so that we look down on others. Admiring ourselves also tends to become a hidden motive for what we do, an ulterior aim that secretly pleases us more than our ostensive motives. So although there may be a sense in which we can legitimately admire ourselves (perhaps respect would be a better word), we need to be on our guard lest we be carried away by it.

✷ Sunday

Even if no one else notices what we do,
we notice.

✷ Monday

Though we feel shame when we catch ourselves
with inordinate self-admiration, we secretly love
to indulge in it.

✷ Tuesday

It is as difficult to love the unlovable as it is
to avoid quietly congratulating ourselves
for doing so.

✷ Wednesday

One of the secrets we most fear to admit is how
much we admire ourselves.

✷ Thursday

Who can resist congratulating herself for being
gracious to someone who has hurt her?

✷ Friday

When our achievements increase, so does the
temptation to excessive self-admiration.

✷ Saturday

The subtlest taint on virtue occurs when
self-admiration energizes it.

Week 17

Justifying Ourselves

When we are looking for admiration, we are trying to justify ourselves. This means that we are trying to make ourselves appear right and good. The idea is contained in the story of the Pharisee and the tax collector (Lk 18:9-14 *NRSV*). The Pharisee went to the temple and prayed, "God, I thank you that I am not like other people: thieves, rogues, adulterers, or even like this tax collector." The tax collector, however, standing at a distance, prayed, "God, be merciful to me, a sinner." It was the tax collector, Jesus declared, who went home truly justified.

The trouble with the Pharisee was that he was trying to justify himself instead of letting God do so. He was congratulating himself on being virtuous, unlike the swindler whom he spotted in a dark corner of the Temple.

This story illustrates the human tendency to find justification either in the wrong things or in the wrong way. It is a tendency that pervades nearly all that we do.

✺ Sunday

The lure of self-justification is as subtle
as it is irresistible.

✺ Monday

Feeling justified because of the rightness of our
religious stance undermines the genuineness of
the stance.

✺ Tuesday

The amount of energy we expend trying to win
others' favor is a measure of our drive to justify
our existence.

✺ Wednesday

Some people use popularity and wealth to justify
themselves; others imagine themselves doing so.

✺ Thursday

Little escapes our use for self-justification:
clothes, jobs, even character traits
and sacrificial activities.

✺ Friday

If possessing God's love makes us think we are
distinguished, it is not love we have,
but feelings of distinction.

✺ Saturday

When we succeed at something that matters, we
feel that our whole existence is validated.

Week 18

Pretending

Ever since we were little, we have pretended. In childhood our pretending was innocent—we dressed up as one of our heroes and acted as we imagined she or he would. Our adult pretending can also be innocent, as when we play charades or perform in plays. More likely it will be less than innocent. We have learned that others do not react well to sadness or discouragement, so we pretend to be happy and optimistic. We have come to fear the disapproval others display when we act in ways that do not fit well with their expectations, which causes us to modify our behavior. In religious contexts we have discovered that we must make efforts to appear religious even though we may not feel like being religious all the time.

It may be that some of our adult pretending is needed in order to keep social interactions running smoothly. More often, though, it serves only as a means of avoiding disapproval or obtaining admiration.

☀ Sunday

We pretend to be good because we fear others' disapproval; others pretend to be good because they fear our disapproval.

☀ Monday

Sometimes both our public and private postures are at variance with what we really are.

☀ Tuesday

Though we are fiercely averse to pretending, we are just as ardently gratified with it.

☀ Wednesday

We like to imagine ourselves better looking, more popular—and more spiritual—than we really are.

☀ Thursday

It is easy to conceive the idea of wearing a mask but not easy to picture our own masks.

☀ Friday

We like to think that our motives are as unfeigned as our actions appear to be.

☀ Saturday

Using religious language in order to fit in with others who also use it is sometimes easier than using it honestly and genuinely.

Week 19

Appearing Virtuous

We want to be known for our moral virtues. This is especially true in contexts that hold certain kinds of virtues in high esteem, such as schools, communities of faith, or other groups held together by a common aim.

In such contexts the pressure to conform to the group's ideals is felt by the members of the group. They do not want to be too different from others in the group. So they make sure that the group regards them in the right way. If they belong to a group that values studiousness, they will talk about their studies to others in the group. If the group of which they are a part values compassion, kindness, harmony, and gentleness, then they will see to it that these virtues are prominently displayed in their actions.

It is not true, of course, that we want only to appear virtuous without actually being virtuous. We usually want both. Sometimes the desire to be virtuous is in the foreground, and sometimes the desire only to be known as virtuous is more prominent. It is the latter that we must watch out for.

✸ Sunday

The thought of how we appear to others often moves us more than the thought of how we appear to God.

✸ Monday

Virtue attracts us both for its own sake and for the admiration it brings.

✸ Tuesday

If all we want when we exhibit love is for others to notice what we do, then it is not love at all.

✸ Wednesday

We use our public character as armor for protection against others' knowledge of our real motives.

✸ Thursday

When expectations for virtue are high, we quickly learn how to appear virtuous.

✸ Friday

It is superhumanly hard not to notice others observing our virtue.

✸ Saturday

One lesson for which we do not need a school is how to obtain others' admiration by appearing good.

Week 20

The Real Thing

One of our deepest desires is to be authentic. We want to be "real and genuine." We do not want our virtue to be counterfeit or our love to be false. When we encounter a person whom we suspect is counterfeit, we are instinctively repulsed. Our greatest admiration is directed toward those whom we regard as sincere and unaffected.

In spite of this desire for authenticity, something in us pushes us to put on a good front. It is easier, after all, to appear virtuous than actually to be virtuous, and sometimes more rewarding. We like being admired and we especially like public acclaim.

The struggle to be real involves uncovering the ways in which we put on a false display. Our aim is to be who we appear to be—to have the compassion our actions show and the faith our religious practices exhibit.

✹ Sunday

It is easier to be a copy of a spiritual person than to be a real one.

✹ Monday

Adopting a faith stance so as to become acceptable to those in a church is like wearing the right clothes to church—both are motivated by "the thing to do."

✹ Tuesday

When we love only in order to be loved, our love is merely manipulation.

✹ Wednesday

We know that the ability to talk in religious ways is different from living in these ways, yet we unconsciously mistake the one for the other.

✹ Thursday

If the respect we have toward others depends solely on their social status, it is not real respect.

✹ Friday

The quickest way faith dies is by conforming unthinkingly to others' expectations regarding it.

✹ Saturday

If we revel in the thought that our spiritual experiences are more profound than others', it is likely that they are not.

Week 21

Sly and Crafty Enemies

Sören Kierkegaard, a Christian philosopher, once observed that "doubt is sly and guileful, not at all loud-mouthed and defiant, as it is sometimes proclaimed to be; it is unassuming and crafty, not brash and presumptuous." To this he added, "and the more unassuming it is, the more dangerous it is."

This is right on target. A sly and crafty enemy is more dangerous than a brash and presumptuous one because we cannot see it. A guileful enemy weasels its way into our minds without our suspecting. It affects our motives, changes our desires, and redirects our energy in disquieting ways. We need to be on our guard against such enemies more than we do against public assaults on faith and love.

Here are some instances of this kind of snare.

❊ Sunday

It is just as possible to flee from God by "being good" as it is by being bad.

❊ Monday

If we have an instinct for discovering hypocrites and a special dislike of them, we are likely to be one ourselves.

❊ Tuesday

Thinking that everyone needs divine forgiveness easily becomes a replacement for being aware that we ourselves need it.

❊ Wednesday

Addiction to envy and greed is as deadly as addiction to alcohol or drugs.

❊ Thursday

Society's admiration of active, fast-moving people draws us unwittingly into mindless motion.

❊ Friday

The love of love sometimes stimulates us to love and sometimes substitutes for love.

❊ Saturday

Unconsciously identifying with a community of faith can give us the illusion of having faith.

Week 22

The Lure of Imagination

Imagination is both enriching and injurious. It is enriching when we use it to discover fresh ways of loving, enlarge our vision, and uncover new sources of goodness and magnificence. Most of us need more of this imaginativeness.

Imagination is injurious when it prevents us from having genuine love and faith. It can do this by making us think we are more loving than we really are, blinding us to suffering, or presenting us with subtle ways of appearing virtuous. It does not do this brashly and openly, but shrewdly and deviously. We sometimes catch ourselves indulging in its schemes, but normally our imagination operates unhindered. To nab it takes as much cleverness as it itself employs.

✺ Sunday

Imaginary faith is much more
pleasant—and safer—than real faith.

✺ Monday

Little is sweeter than imagining ourselves being
much admired.

✺ Tuesday

A retreat into imagination is especially alluring
when life becomes too strenuous.

✺ Wednesday

An imaginary beggar does not stink;
a real beggar does.

✺ Thursday

If no one notices our goodness, we imagine
someone doing so.

✺ Friday

Our secret prayer rooms are sometimes filled with
imaginary spectators.

✺ Saturday

It is possible to fall in love so much with the idea
of love that we think it is real love.

Week 23

Busyness

We live in a culture that is obsessed with action. Always, everywhere, people are doing things. Rarely does anyone sit quietly for long and simply do nothing.

It is, of course, a good thing to be active and engaged. At the same time, incessant activity affects us adversely. It prevents us from thinking about the direction of our lives. It becomes a substitute for sorting through our emotions. It blinds us to what really counts.

Pascal once declared that we go through our whole life hustling and bustling, diverting ourselves from important issues. If we can break through this hustle and bustle, we might be able to catch a glimpse of the eternal.

☀ Sunday

Busyness dulls us to new possibilities.

☀ Monday

If we overload ourselves with worthy activities,
we will soon want to give them all up.

☀ Tuesday

In a culture of industriousness, nonproductive
solitude is regarded as having little value.

☀ Wednesday

Though we complain about being too busy, we
often prefer it that way.

☀ Thursday

Some people use alcohol, drugs, and sex to
escape thinking about their true condition; others
use books, games, and travel.

☀ Friday

The easiest, though not the best, remedy for
boredom is to bury ourselves in activity.

☀ Saturday

The charm of busyness is its diversion.

Week 24

A Bundle of Desires

A quick inspection of our inner selves reveals an assortment of desires and passions. If we were to take an inventory of them all, we would be surprised at how many we have. This is as it should be, of course. We are extraordinarily complex creatures.

The question we need to ask is whether these desires and passions take us toward the eternal or whether they crowd out our pursuit of the eternal. It is not the quantity of our desires that should concern us, but their direction. The tragic truth is that many of our desires take us the wrong way.

Here are a few that need to be worked on.

✸ Sunday

Sometimes we prefer worry to inner peace.

✸ Monday

Some people wrestle with pride more
than they do with self-denigration, while for
others it is the reverse.

✸ Tuesday

Every time we succumb to lust or gluttony, we
weaken our resolve to resist them.

✸ Wednesday

Some desires need to be resisted, while others
need to be crowded out by stronger desires.

✸ Thursday

Sometimes we get as much pleasure in belittling
ourselves as we do in magnifying ourselves.

✸ Friday

If our self-worth depends on the things we own,
we will clutch them desperately.

✸ Saturday

We often hold on to certain attitudes and
emotions just as tightly as we do to possessions.

Week 25

Ulterior Aims

Most of what we do has more than one motive. For example, a person may go to medical school both to fulfill a childhood ambition and to serve others. Or a person may go to medical school ostensibly to serve others but really to obtain high social status. In the first case, we would not say that the person has an ulterior motive, though we would say this in the second. This second case is the one we need to guard against. Our ostensive motives should be uncontaminated by ulterior motives.

Unfortunately, ulterior motives are often hidden. So we must lay them bare and expose them for what they are.

Here are a few prominent ones.

☼ Sunday

The drive to succeed may come partly from the desire to do well and partly from the desire to feed one's ego.

☼ Monday

It is one thing to have the sense of loving well; it is another to love in order to have this sense.

☼ Tuesday

If we value the attention others give us because of their status, it is not simply the attention we value.

☼ Wednesday

Play ceases to be play when it becomes infected with the need to prove we are better than others.

☼ Thursday

We are scarcely able to do anything distinctive without thinking of someone to whom we will brag about it.

☼ Friday

The sweetest feature of doing something good is often the commendation we give ourselves for it.

☼ Saturday

Genuine goodness increases admiration from others—and the temptation to display the goodness for the admiration.

Week 26

Inner Temptations

When we think of temptations, we usually picture sweets, excess food or alcohol, and illegitimate sex. "Don't tempt me," we say, meaning that we are trying to avoid some overt action. Inner temptations, however, are often overlooked. We rarely notice that we can indulge ourselves in inner states as much as we do in overt actions. We can bask in apathy, luxuriate in greed, and wallow in envy as easily as we can consume an extra doughnut.

The reason inner temptations are important is that if we succumb to them, we undermine our pursuit of eternity. This pursuit is as much a matter of what is inside us as of what we do.

Here are some distinct inner temptations.

✲ Sunday

There is much gratification in relishing critical thoughts about others.

✲ Monday

The chief danger in thinking that our spiritual experiences are profound is that we will regard them as being superior to the experiences of others.

✲ Tuesday

If our prayers are filled with requests for ourselves, they are evidence more of egocentricity than of spirituality.

✲ Wednesday

Believing we are admired for our religious activities tempts us to believe that God admires us for them.

✲ Thursday

We grudgingly acknowledge virtue in others but are highly impressed with our own.

✲ Friday

The impulse to rely more on our possessions than on God grows as we obtain more possessions.

✲ Saturday

The pleasure we get when we use people for our own ends is of one kind, and the pleasure we have in loving them unconditionally is of another.

Third Quarter

Becoming New

It is time to look at the means we can use to move beyond the obstacles described in the last quarter. Unfortunately, no one simple formula can tell us how. Life is too complex for that. When we think we have banished one obstacle, another rears up. While we are battling it, the first creeps back in. There seems to be no end of hurdles to overcome in pursuing the eternal.

Still, some simple truths can be stated: Allow God to love you. Keep faith alive. Give love away. Stay focused. Look for what is beautiful in people.

Perhaps the single truth behind these admonitions is that we must undergo a basic change. We must reorient our desires so that the obstacles no longer tempt us. Our passions must change so that they are directed toward love and faith. We must, in short, become the kind of persons who crave the eternal. The weeks in this quarter describe some of the ways we can become transformed in this way.

Week 27

Being Open to Grace

When we open ourselves to God's freely offered love, we exchange one set of desires for another. We give up our need to justify ourselves and be admired. We let go of our impulse to congratulate ourselves and of our inclination to criticize ourselves. Our love is freed of ulterior motives and we give without thought of return. We are also freed of compulsions. We wake up from indifference, and our resistance to goodness is melted.

Something about God's grace attracts us. When we experience it, we feel elated and want to keep on experiencing it. We relish its presence with a quiet thankfulness.

☀ Sunday

The core of taking in God's grace is letting go of our attachment to self-justification.

☀ Monday

When we allow ourselves to be loved by God, we give up our consuming passion to get ahead.

☀ Tuesday

To be permeated by God's grace means that we do not overtly act in spiritual ways while covertly wanting wide recognition for our spirituality.

☀ Wednesday

The most difficult task a successful person faces is remaining open to God's grace. It is also the most difficult task an unsuccessful person faces.

☀ Thursday

Without fresh experiences of grace, we are likely to be controlled by our untamed impulses.

☀ Friday

The mere remembrance of prior experiences of grace awakens a desire for more.

☀ Saturday

If we were to regard God's grace as an unexpected gift, we might skip and twirl with spontaneous gratitude.

Week 28

Wrestling With Grace

Although God's grace is freely given, it is extraordinarily difficult to accept. We want to make something of ourselves apart from grace. We like to be admired for what we do. We are uncomfortable being given love by someone whom we do not have to pay back. We imagine we have to earn our good status with God. We do not want to admit that we cannot save ourselves.

These passions run deep in us. They are the driving force of much of our lives. So if we are to take in God's grace, we will have to wrestle with it. We will need to acknowledge the hold these passions have on us and let grace slowly lessen that hold.

✲ Sunday

Our ceaseless striving for admiration deadens us
to God's grace.

✲ Monday

We often wrestle more intensely temptation
after we take in God's grace then we did
before we took it in.

✲ Tuesday

Our grasp of God's grace is sometimes sure,
sometimes precarious.

✲ Wednesday

The only real mercy is probing, burning mercy.

✲ Thursday

Receiving undeserved love is like getting
a gift from someone whom we have let down—
we want to give it back.

✲ Friday

Little undermines our openness to God's grace
more than the thought that we are decent persons
who are worthy of God's respect.

✲ Saturday

Grace cannot heal us until we recognize our
self-inflicted wounds, which we are loath to do.

Week 29

Allowing Ourselves to Be Loved

Being loved, we might think, is easy. We simply accept it in the same way we accept a gift. In this, though, lies the rub. We might feel that we are not worthy of being loved. Or we might feel that we have to pay back the one who loves us, which turns the love into a transaction. We might also be afraid that we will have to reveal our secrets to the one who loves us.

These hurdles also exist when it comes to allowing ourselves to be loved by God. Although God always loves us, we must get past the hurdles if we are to take in God's love.

☼ Sunday

The one thing harder than loving is allowing ourselves to be loved.

☼ Monday

"It is better to give than to receive"—but not if giving is a way of avoiding the discomfort of receiving.

☼ Tuesday

Nothing stings more than to be given undeserved love.

☼ Wednesday

It is not easy to allow ourselves to be loved if we are consumed by despair.

☼ Thursday

Letting God love us means letting God know the secret places in our hearts.

☼ Friday

We often feel so unnerved by selfless love that our first, and sometimes last, impulse is to reject it.

☼ Saturday

We are not selfish for wanting more love, provided we do not want to use it for anything.

Week 30

Letting Go

In order to be open to God's grace, we must let go of some of our dearest desires. We must give up our craving to justify our existence in false ways. We must abandon our appetite to be better than everyone else. We must relinquish our hold on the urge to belittle ourselves.

Letting go of these desires involves surrendering ourselves to God. We let go of the cravings and turn ourselves over to the one who gives grace. Our aim should be to let grace permeate our entire being. We need to be open to grace both in our conscious life and in the deepest recesses of our personality.

☀ Sunday

We cannot be open to God's grace if we constantly demean ourselves.

☀ Monday

To be free from the need to compare oneself to others is the mark of a grace-filled person.

☀ Tuesday

Taking in God's grace requires us to unveil our secret failings to God.

☀ Wednesday

It is not enough simply to want to be free from our addictions; we must be desperate.

☀ Thursday

We can become open to God's grace only when we give up our efforts to vindicate ourselves.

☀ Friday

If we need to criticize others to feel secure, we also need a heavy dose of God's grace.

☀ Saturday

To experience God's forgiveness without feeling that we must do something to earn it is as difficult as it is liberating.

Week 31

Gaining a New Identity

In letting go of the desires that undermine our reception of God's grace, we obtain a new identity. These desires have been so much a part of us that they have formed our self-concept. We picture ourselves as persons who are admired and respected; we conceive ourselves to be better than others in certain ways.

There is a sure test to tell whether these desires are part of our identity: imagine ourselves without them and see what remains. If nothing does, then it is these desires that form our self-concept. In letting go of them, therefore, our concept of ourselves is shattered. In its place, we acquire a new self-image. We become one who is loved by God and one whose controlling desire is to love God.

✹ Sunday

A self-identity based solely on accomplishments crumbles when we take in God's grace.

✹ Monday

Obtaining our worth from God's grace frees us from the need to show others how good we are.

✹ Tuesday

No question requires more courage than, "How can I become new?"

✹ Wednesday

Grace frees us from brooding on the dark parts of our past.

✹ Thursday

Constantly trying to convince ourselves of our worth demonstrates that we possess a self-identity that is based more on performance than on God's grace.

✹ Friday

If maintaining an image of ourselves as a well-respected person consumes us, we have not yet let God's grace work its way into the deepest parts of our lives.

✹ Saturday

The most tortuous—and most liberating— transition is from self-justification to grace's justification.

Week 32

Accepting Ourselves

The one person we find most difficult to accept is ourselves. Self-doubt begins in our teen years, when it torments us, and travels through life with us. We doubt whether anyone else likes us. We think our bodies are ill-formed. We wonder whether we are any good at anything (though as compensation we remind ourselves that we are better than others at some things). Sometimes self-doubt turns into self-criticism or even self-hate.

When we take in God's grace, we can accept ourselves much better. It would be nice to be able to say that with God's grace we can fully accept ourselves. This is true in theory, but in actuality, self-doubt and self-criticism never entirely go away. What grace does, however, is offer us a way to ease these distressing sentiments. Our new identity as one loved by God makes us better able to live peacefully with ourselves.

❂ Sunday

If we adopted God's stance toward us, we probably would treat ourselves with a good deal more compassion than we normally do.

❂ Monday

Those who delight in the significant accomplishments of others without feeling resentment know that their own worth is not diminished by others' successes.

❂ Tuesday

It is better to believe in ourselves and run the risk of conceit than it is to degrade ourselves and live in miserable self-hate.

❂ Wednesday

Inner exploration not accompanied by self-acceptance invariably leads to unremitting despair.

❂ Thursday

We do not need constant distraction when we accept ourselves.

❂ Friday

Nothing eats at our inner contentment more than a keen sense of unworth.

❂ Saturday

Too much self-love makes for inordinate self-esteem; too little makes for self-loathing.

Week 33

Acquiring Single-Minded Faith

Children have a single-minded faith. It contains no contaminants or ulterior motives. It trusts purely and simply. And it comes easily and naturally to them.

A childlike faith does not, unfortunately, come easily to us adults, for we have emotional baggage we must shed and alien drives we must blunt before our faith can become single-minded. We have been betrayed, so that distrust is sometimes more natural for us than trust. We have seen the ways of the world and found them more attractive than the ways of the eternal. We have learned to use others in various ways, one of which, paradoxically, is by having a faith for which we believe other people of faith will regard us highly.

Though we cannot return to the naive innocence of a child's faith, we can work toward a "knowing innocence"—a simplicity that knows what we must work through to acquire a pure faith.

☀ Sunday

Absorbing God's gentle love draws us to
single-minded faith.

☀ Monday

We cannot truly worship God if all we want from
God is for him to satisfy our needs.

☀ Tuesday

Using religious activities to obtain recognition is
just as easy as using secular activities to obtain it.

☀ Wednesday

It is better consciously to pray, "Free me from my
lust, but not yet," than to pray for freedom from
lust without recognizing our reluctance to have
that freedom.

☀ Thursday

Humility in an accomplished person is as
admirable as it is difficult.

☀ Friday

To mourn the loss of childlike faith is to begin to
recapture it.

☀ Saturday

When we know we are loved, we do not
constantly need to seek others' admiration.

Week 34

Sustaining Faith

Faith is a gift from God, it is sometimes said. This is true. But it is just as true that we must work to sustain it. Doubt hits us at odd moments, and we wonder whether our faith is correct. Our religious habits become mechanical and lifeless, causing faith to become dead and inert. We become more attracted to possessions than to faith, and faith shrinks. A vague restlessness overcomes us, making faith waver.

There is no one remedy for a sagging faith. And what works on one occasion may not work on another. One thing is sure: if we do not attend to our faith, it will slip away.

☀ Sunday

The danger in doubting our faith is that it will be undermined; the danger in not doubting it is that it will be counterfeit.

☀ Monday

The restlessness that feeds faith is a striving restlessness.

☀ Tuesday

One mark of genuine faith is the willingness to associate with those who have less social standing than we do.

☀ Wednesday

Whole-hearted faith is like the absorbed interest of a child at play.

☀ Thursday

If faith makes us feel distinguished, it is not faith.

☀ Friday

Our own hidden motives undermine our faith more than does others' overt opposition.

☀ Saturday

Sometimes simply going through the motions of having faith gets us through a dry period and sometimes it dulls us.

Week 35

Keeping Faith Passionate

Without passion, faith goes flat. This, in fact, is true of everything. If our interest in a project flags, the project itself will die. If our emotional investment in a friendship lessens, the friendship will deteriorate.

The passion faith needs does not have to be at a constant high pitch. Indeed, it is impossible to sustain intense passion for very long. Moreover, if we let our faith rely only on episodes of intense passion, it tends to become limp between such episodes.

What faith needs is a calm and steady passion. This kind of passion persists when intense passion has died out. It keeps faith alive and ongoing.

✪ Sunday

Spiritual fervor requires as much dogged persistence as it does enthusiasm.

✪ Monday

Quiet convictions in tranquil settings move us as much as decisive encounters in emotional contexts.

✪ Tuesday

Sometimes the only way to dissipate spiritual numbness is to be shaken up.

✪ Wednesday

We cannot maintain a continuous "high," but we can have long periods of quiet delight.

✪ Thursday

Without infusions of freshness, weariness easily turns into indifference.

✪ Friday

Habits of piety can deaden faith, but they can also keep it alive.

✪ Saturday

Spiritual vitality is sometimes passionate and sometimes serene.

Week 36

Being in a Community of Grace

The groups to which we belong can be sources of admiration and self-justification, unless they are communities of grace. In a community of grace, acceptance is not based on status or prestige. It is given without regard to the standing of the recipient, and it is received without regard to the position of the giver.

Our subterranean self operates in such a subtle and dogged way that we need each other in our efforts to deal with it. We need each other's grace in order to accept ourselves, to keep faith single-minded, and to let go of our drive to be admired. Tangible expressions of grace—a warm smile, a touch—go a long way in excising the ungraced motives that lie deep within.

✸ Sunday

When we are responsive to God's grace, we are inclined to treat others with the same grace.

✸ Monday

The best gifts are our time and interest.

✸ Tuesday

The attitude we should have toward people whom we regard as hypocrites is the attitude we would want people to have toward us if they were to regard us as hypocrites.

✸ Wednesday

To look at others with kind eyes is to give them an irreplaceable gift.

✸ Thursday

In an atmosphere of grace, we feel safe admitting what ordinarily we do not disclose to anyone.

✸ Friday

It is better to love and fumble than to prevent the fumble by not loving.

✸ Saturday

There is little more warming than to be with those who delight in our presence.

Week 37

Recognizing the Wounded

If we regard others solely from the outside, we will have one stance toward them, but if we regard them from the inside, we will have another. We will view them as stumbling searchers who are looking for meaning. We will picture them ardently striving for inner peace. We will see them struggling to salve painful emotions.

It is difficult to regard others in these ways, because they rarely reveal their inner selves to us. Still, those inner selves exist, and they are like our own—wounded, needing love, and trying to make sense of life.

When we see others as wounded, we are prompted to act toward them in ways we want others to act toward our bruised selves. We are moved to give them the grace we ourselves need.

☀ Sunday

Tenderly to touch another's wound is to heal it.

☀ Monday

If we think of those who are proud and conceited as individuals who are hurting and need to be loved, we are more likely actually to love them.

☀ Tuesday

Few of us imagine that others have deep wounds that need healing.

☀ Wednesday

Sometimes a happy face comes from a happy heart and sometimes it masks a wounded heart.

☀ Thursday

The proper response to those who hide their inner pain with a public display of virtue is to admit that we do the same.

☀ Friday

We do not truly know another person until we know their tragedies.

☀ Saturday

It is not "above average" or "below average" by which we should categorize others, but "wounded and in need of grace."

Week 38

Giving Grace

When we give grace, we convey to others that we take them as they are. We can do this with words that carry a connotation of gracious acceptance, or we can do it by refraining from using words that provoke a defensive attitude, such as unpleasant teasing. We can also convey grace by our general demeanor, as when we adopt a receptive posture toward others—by looking into their eyes with gentle kindness, by showing that we enjoy their presence, by radiating emotional warmth toward them.

This grace stance does not come easily, for we normally are so wrapped up in ourselves that we cannot give much to others. And we often base our regard for them on their social standing. Giving grace requires that we let go of our excessive concern for ourselves and look upon others as ones who need grace. To do this, we must undergo a radical change of heart.

✹ Sunday

An invitation to love arrives whenever we
encounter another person.

✹ Monday

The kind of love we should want to give is the
kind of love we crave to receive.

✹ Tuesday

The best—and most difficult—place to give grace
is in one's family.

✹ Wednesday

When we identify with others' turmoil, they can
see in our eyes that we do.

✹ Thursday

True listening gives grace.

✹ Friday

We cannot empathize if we are not alert to
others' inner pain.

✹ Saturday

To delight in another's presence requires us to
have a need-free stance toward them.

Week 39

Receiving Grace

It is one thing to be given grace and it is another actually to accept it. We might not be in the right frame of mind to accept grace. We might use it to puff up our ego. Or we might not recognize what is given to us as grace.

To receive grace, we must take in its unconditional acceptance of us. Doing this, though, does not come easy, because we want others to base their regard for us on our personal qualities and status. So when we are given grace, we tend to turn it into admiration. Or we reject it outright.

Receiving grace requires as much of a change of heart as does giving grace. We must give up our drive to expand our ego and look upon ourselves as ones who need grace.

✺ Sunday

Sometimes we receive love with welcome delight; other times we distance ourselves from it.

✺ Monday

We cannot receive grace from others if we think of them as inferior or superior to us.

✺ Tuesday

The person who eagerly devours another's gratitude is desperate for admiration; the person who graciously accepts gratitude does not need admiration to sustain herself.

✺ Wednesday

We often find it harder to accept praise than to give it.

✺ Thursday

To accept a gift as a gift, we must first be able to accept ourselves.

✺ Friday

The memory of a friend's touch is nearly as warm as the touch itself.

✺ Saturday

Receiving a gift can stir up latent feelings of unworthiness, but it can also dispel them.

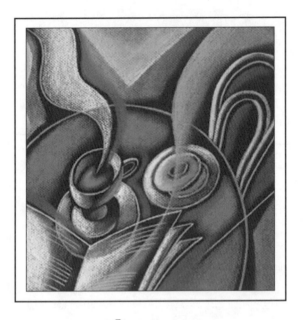

Fourth Quarter

Moving Toward the Eternal

In earlier centuries, pilgrimages were more common than they are in our own century. In nineteenth-century Russia, solitary pilgrims walked from place to place, working and praying as they traveled. During the Middle Ages, groups of pilgrims made their way to Jerusalem from various European countries. Most of us in the United States, however, do not find the idea of going on a pilgrimage appealing. It is a thing of the past, for people who travel slowly or for those who want to move to a new land.

It is time to resurrect the idea. Moving toward the eternal is like being on a pilgrimage. It has a goal, it has means to the goal, and it is like wandering in a wilderness. We do not always go in a straight path toward our goal. At the same time, we recognize landmarks along the way. We know that overall we are moving in the right direction. And we exult in the fact that even though we are not at the end of our journey, we experience bits and pieces of what it will be like when we are. This quarter describes some of these bits and pieces.

Week 40

Reflecting on Goodness

We need to reflect more on the goodness in life. That is, we need to hold it in our attention more, be glad for it, delight in it, even revel in it and celebrate it.

Two obstacles hamper our doing so. The first is that it is more exciting to gape at sin and evil, misfortune and catastrophe. We would rather read about these in newspapers and hear about them on the evening news than listen to accounts of everyday good. The latter are frequently boring and dull, we think. The second obstacle is the press of daily duties. We are so consumed by all we must do that the mere thought of what is good eludes us. We have to attend to this and that, now and all day, and we do not break the rush of thoughts for a moment of contemplation. If we did, we might find ourselves transformed.

✺ Sunday

Focusing our attention on God draws us to God.

✺ Monday

Being haunted by the memory of an evil deadens;
treasuring the memory of a good quickens.

✺ Tuesday

Silence is not restorative if we brood on our
worries during it.

✺ Wednesday

We become what we take in: if we absorb evil,
we become cynical and quarrelsome; if we
assimilate goodness, we become warm and
ungrudging.

✺ Thursday

Constant repetition of religious activity can numb
us to God, but it can also pull us to God.

✺ Friday

We cannot listen to God if all we do is talk to
God.

✺ Saturday

We may take such an active interest in others'
welfare that we do not notice that we have an
inner life that needs attending to.

Week 41

Loving

The one thing everyone needs is to be loved. Those with failure in their lives need to feel accepted. Those with painful memories need support; those who are struggling to make sense of their lives need encouragement; those with guilt need forgiveness; those who are battling low self-esteem need shoring up. Love does all of these things. It accepts, supports, encourages, forgives, and shores up.

If everyone needs to be loved more, it follows that other people need to love more. We, of course, are those other people. When we love, people sense that their lives are worthwhile. They are encouraged and feel accepted. They can deal with failure and disabilities. With our loving, people are enabled to lead richer lives.

☼ Sunday

The best love comes from an overflowing heart.

☼ Monday

More courage is required to love than to walk two blocks through a gang-infested territory at night.

☼ Tuesday

Finding untainted love is as exhilarating as it is surprising.

☼ Wednesday

People change more when we love them without trying to change them than when we actively try to change them.

☼ Thursday

Our delight in another's presence exhibits itself on our faces.

☼ Friday

If we have never been the recipient of real love, we may have to look for people who will love us before looking for people to love.

☼ Saturday

The core of love is to be present to another without trying to get something for ourselves.

Week 42

Listening

Listening is one way we can love others. It is, in fact, a very significant way. Listening conveys our interest in others. It says, "I am giving my time to you now, unreservedly." We show by our action that we regard others as having worth. Those who are listened to feel this interest and sense the unreserved gift of time. They also feel understood. When we listen, we sympathetically absorb others' thoughts and feelings, sometimes their deepest emotions.

Like other loving, listening does not come easy. It requires skill. We must maintain eye contact, ask the right questions, and demonstrate that we are continuing to listen during long stretches of talk. It also requires setting aside our own concerns and focusing on those of others. Doing this is often harder than we suppose, because our natural proclivity is to talk, especially about ourselves. Good listening requires both practice and an inner change.

☼ Sunday

Everyone craves to be listened to, but only a few are willing to listen.

☼ Monday

A person who is genuinely interested in what others do and feel is likely to be a good listener.

☼ Tuesday

The only way to listen is to stop talking.

☼ Wednesday

Listening feeds a starving heart.

☼ Thursday

A true listener temporarily effaces his or her own need to be listened to.

☼ Friday

Wanting only attention from a conversation makes listening impossible.

☼ Saturday

Five minutes of pure listening often has an incalculable effect.

Week 43

Confessing and Forgiving

None of us wants to admit that we have gone wrong. Our need to feel right and good is so strong that we shrink from the very idea of confessing our lapses. We think we will lose our standing in others' eyes. And we may.

Forgiving is also not our natural inclination. We like to harbor resentment toward those who have wronged us. We like to believe we are better than they are. Forgiving them would dissolve the resentment and undo our supposed superiority.

What we need is to be in a setting in which confessing and forgiving are accepted and encouraged. In such a setting, people do not fear confessing, for they know they will be forgiven. And those who have been wronged, though hurt and resentful, work on extending forgiveness.

☀ Sunday

Without gracious acceptance, confession is squelched.

☀ Monday

Sometimes it takes a decade to forgive a grievous hurt.

☀ Tuesday

When we admit our secrets to others, they feel safe in admitting their secrets to us.

☀ Wednesday

Those who refrain from denigrating others when they fail are silent bearers of grace.

☀ Thursday

We cannot forgive if we view those who have wronged us with condescension.

☀ Friday

Our sharpest shame comes from discovering that we ourselves have done what we detest in others.

☀ Saturday

A candid confession prompts one in return.

Week 44

Living Together in Love

In his great novel *The Brothers Karamazov*, Fyodor Dostoevsky has a doctor say, "The more I love humanity in general, the less I love men in particular, I mean, separately, as separate individuals. In my dreams, I am very often passionately determined to serve humanity, . . . and yet I'm quite incapable of living with anyone in one room for two days together, and I know that from experience."

The doctor has discovered that it is much easier to love people as an abstraction or in one's imagination. Up close, they bother us. They get in our way and say hurtful things to us. Their idiosyncrasies irritate us.

At the same time, little enriches us more than to live together in love. Doing so encourages us to strive for our highest. It teaches us patience and generosity. Through it, we become able to confess and forgive. Without it, our lives would be much impoverished.

❁ Sunday

Though loving the whole world in our
imagination is easier than loving a particular
person in reality, it is not nearly as exciting.

❁ Monday

If we are too numbed by daily routine to love,
then we are, indeed, too numb.

❁ Tuesday

Those who love well freely admit their flaws.

❁ Wednesday

We will not look for opportunities to love if all
we want is to get ahead.

❁ Thursday

The truest test of real love is whether we can talk
gently to someone who has hurt us.

❁ Friday

To look at others with kind eyes is to give them a
great gift.

❁ Saturday

Little is more dismaying than to realize
we have needlessly hurt someone about whom
we care deeply.

Week 45

Shrinking the Expansive Ego

G. K. Chesterton once remarked that the greatest discovery we can make is that there are other people. His point is that we are so wrapped up in our own concerns that we are oblivious to those of others. Our expansive egos blind us. They make us think that the only thing that counts is what matters to us.

But other people count, too. If we could shrink our egos, we would come to realize this fact. We would become aware of others' feelings, their disappointments and sufferings, delights and joys. We would notice, as Chesterton declared, that they exist.

Noticing this, paradoxically, would enlarge us. We would experience a wider array of significant human emotions. We would connect to others at a deeper level. We might even find that our lives have more meaning.

✪ Sunday

Those who let go of their grip on the fat,
relentless ego are able to give need-free love.

✪ Monday

Although all of us need to love better, we also
need to take care of ourselves better.

✪ Tuesday

Too much self-interest blinds us to others' beauty.

✪ Wednesday

A sure way to lose our self-absorption is to attend
to another's suffering.

✪ Thursday

We are neither wholly self-centered nor wholly
selfless.

✪ Friday

We cannot be compassionate if we are
preoccupied with ourselves.

✪ Saturday

Those with true humility do not exalt themselves,
nor do they demean themselves.

Week 46

Moving Beyond the Self

Something in us is dissatisfied with a completely self-seeking life. We sense that it is narrow and ultimately unfulfilling. If we love only to be admired and given homage, we feel hollow and empty. And if we give only to get something in return, we feel as if we have missed something vital.

Basically, we want to move beyond ourselves. Perhaps it is more accurate to say that we long for this. Although we dearly like living only for ourselves, we are discontent with it as well.

We can move beyond ourselves in a number of ways. We can praise God self-forgetfully. We can look for the good in others. We can love without regard to what we get from doing so.

☀ Sunday

Genuinely self-forgetful praise of God is
profoundly fulfilling, though this is the result
of the praise and not the aim of it.

☀ Monday

We can love others rightly only when we let go of
our infatuation with ourselves.

☀ Tuesday

Those who truly love do not wait for
opportunities to love; they look for them.

☀ Wednesday

A loving person does not insist that people notice
her.

☀ Thursday

An active carer searches others' faces for signs of
distress and happiness.

☀ Friday

Love: the more we get, the more we want to give
it away.

☀ Saturday

The true "reward" of loving is delight in the
loving itself and not what we get from the loving.

Week 47

Observing Moral Beauty

When we discover that other people exist, we experience their acts of kindness and everyday triumphs as instances of moral beauty. We react to these instances in the same way we react to marvels of nature—with a keen sense of awe.

This awe might be experienced as a high-pitched exhilaration, as when we first encounter a spectacular mountain scene or magnificent landscape. Or it might be experienced as a steady and calm enjoyment, as when we savor a sunny day with blue skies. Either way, our awe of another's goodness consists of appreciation for it, mixed with esteem and high admiration.

With this awe, our own lives become enriched. Something about taking in goodness graces us with an inner abundance. We become serene and tranquil. Our indifference and bitterness are replaced with rejoicing and celebration.

✪ Sunday

Becoming aware of instances of gentleness,
forgiveness, and compassion makes
life worth living.

✪ Monday

A truly beautiful soul evokes breathtaking awe.

✪ Tuesday

We can see the inner beauty in others only if we
actively look for it.

✪ Wednesday

Those who delight in others' goodness are
themselves good.

✪ Thursday

One who observes love given can be enlivened
as much as one who receives love.

✪ Friday

There is little more heartening than beholding the
goodness in our acquaintances.

✪ Saturday

To notice beauty in others, we must look past the
ways they have fallen.

Week 48

Living Largely

A person who lives in a narrow and constricted way does not actively look for opportunities to love, whereas one who lives in an open and enlarged way never ceases to do so. The first person explores little and takes few risks; the second constantly explores and takes many risks. If we could ward off the first way of living and nourish the second, we would be immeasurably enriched.

It is not, however, easy to become open to life's grand possibilities. We are afraid of sticking out too much. Old habits die hard. Fear of the new is too strong. Most of the time we would rather keep love and goodness at bay.

When we live more largely, we give a great deal, but we also receive a great deal. We are sensitive both to the tragedies others suffer and to the magnificence they possess. We cultivate kindness, generosity, patience, and humility; we pursue what is important and leave behind what is trivial; we welcome all good, loving it more than anything.

✸ Sunday

Most of the magnificence in life attaches to what is ordinary.

✸ Monday

Extravagant giving comes from an expansive heart.

✸ Tuesday

To savor a kindness given to another enriches one's own life.

✸ Wednesday

The largeness of love is both frightening and exhilarating.

✸ Thursday

Living more largely requires eliminating nonessentials.

✸ Friday

Our lives are impoverished without judicious amounts of both delight and sorrow.

✸ Saturday

The real adventures of life take place inside us.

Week 49

Looking for Goodness

When we become alive to goodness, we actively look for it. We do not simply wait for it to appear. That would be like waiting for people to become our friends. If we do not deliberately cultivate friendships, they will never exist. We must work at them. In the same way, if we do not work at acquiring a disposition to recognize goodness, it will never exist. We will remain unaware of goodness even when it appears to us.

It appears to us often, in fact. It resides in the thousand and one events we encounter every day. When God saw that everything he had made was very good (Gen 1:31), it was not just the galaxies and mountains he was looking at. It was the tidbits as well. It was common occurrences like talking and walking, cooking and eating, playing and learning, reading and making.

When, then, we cultivate a disposition to recognize goodness, we become aware of it on numerous occasions. In doing so, we are experiencing a little bit of what God experiences all the time.

☀ Sunday

Looking for goodness requires us to reorient our desires.

☀ Monday

Two people may look at the still, precise reflection of a tree in a pond, but only one may see its beauty.

☀ Tuesday

To be alive to goodness, we must give up our indifference to it.

☀ Wednesday

If we see dirt and ugliness in others, we will treat them with scorn and contempt; if we see beauty, we will act with delight and care.

☀ Thursday

The desire for goodness must be a perpetual hunger or it will die.

☀ Friday

We often notice another's physical beauty more quickly than their inner beauty, and sometimes that is all we notice.

☀ Saturday

Our awe for another's goodness should match our awe for spectacular physical beauty.

Week 50

Staying Vibrant

What can we do to keep ourselves vibrant and alive to goodness? How can we keep from going dead? Here are some ways of doing so.

1. Ask people cosmic questions, such as, "What do you like most about living?" or "How is your life?" and listen intently to their responses.
2. Go to the mountains and let their beauty become etched on your mind.
3. Continue spiritual habits even if doing so feels mechanical.
4. Mix with people who are ethnically different or who are of a lower socio-economic class and listen to their life stories.
5. Give someone a cookie.
6. Blow bubbles at a busy city street intersection.
7. Memorize significant verses in the Bible.
8. Let go of what is trivial.

☀ Sunday

Sometimes our daily tasks numb us to goodness;
sometimes they draw it out.

☀ Monday

Not to care about whether we are wasting our
lives is the supreme indifference.

☀ Tuesday

"Humankind cannot bear very much reality"
(T. S. Eliot), nor can it bear very much unreality.

☀ Wednesday

Without episodes of elation, we are not likely to
escape the dull torpor in which we often live.

☀ Thursday

It is better to be alive than dead, but not by much
if our lives are living deaths.

☀ Friday

"Most people live lives of quiet desperation"
(Henry David Thoreau), part of which is the terror
of admitting that we do.

☀ Saturday

Goodness can enliven a dreary life as much as
wickedness.

Week 51

Finding Meaning

Life would be a sham if we had no hope of finding meaning. The search for meaning has worth, to be sure, but if life is only a search, it is fraudulent. Why should we devote high amounts of energy looking for something we will never find?

We can find meaning. It comes from loving and being loved, giving and receiving grace, acquiring single-minded faith, observing moral beauty, listening, letting go of trivial pursuits, and living together in love.

The paradoxical truth about those who live for eternity is that they both look for meaning and have found it. They yearn for something more, yet possess that for which they yearn. They are empty and full, restless and contented, ever searching yet always finding.

✺ Sunday

Little can subdue our ceaseless strivings more
than delighting in genuine good.

✺ Monday

It is mostly inner obstacles that prevent us from
fulfilling our life dreams.

✺ Tuesday

The remedy for lifeless habits may be to replace
them, but it may also be to infuse them with
freshness.

✺ Wednesday

The one who looks for adventure in everyday
events will never be bored.

✺ Thursday

Observing a single instance of goodness restores
one's sense that life is worth living.

✺ Friday

Without hope, dejection is likely to cripple.

✺ Saturday

Only love, both its giving and receiving,
permanently fills our hollowness.

Week 52

Living for Eternity

To live for eternity means two things: to live for what is truly significant, and to live for what will last beyond the grave. When we die, we are told, the wood, hay, and straw in our lives will be burned, but the gold, silver, and precious stones will remain (1 Cor 3:12-15). The wood, hay, and straw represent our pursuit of trivialities, the monuments we have erected to ourselves, our devotion to piling up excess stuff, our inner addictions. It will hurt to have these burned, because we have loved them and made them part of who we are.

The gold, silver, and precious stones represent our loving and listening, our vibrant faith, our observations of moral beauty, our love of God. When, beyond the grave, we observe that these have remained, we will rejoice that we have made them part of our lives. We will do so partly for their inherent value and partly out of gratitude to the One who has made us for them.

✺ Sunday

Grand visions are worked out in details.

✺ Monday

The best way to keep our desire for eternity from being squeezed out is to make it stronger than every other desire.

✺ Tuesday

The biggest struggle in life is to be good; the biggest tragedy is not to take the struggle seriously.

✺ Wednesday

Quiet radiance is as beautiful as it is rare.

✺ Thursday

Some of our everyday desires obstruct our craving for eternity and some are motivated by it.

✺ Friday

The one who is willing to be interrupted knows where the true business of life lies.

✺ Saturday

Those who never risk loving never really live.

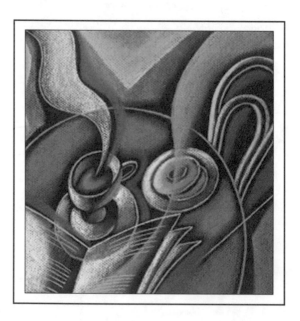

Day 365

Beginning Now

When can we start living for eternity? Right now. Though we cannot instantly adopt all the ways of the eternal, we can do so bit by bit. That, after all, is how anything large and wonderful gets accomplished. Right now we can give someone grace with a kind smile, remember an instance of moral beauty, or take in God's love.

Every moment is a little death—and a little birth.

An author and professor of philosophy
at Trinity College in Deerfield, Illinois,
CLIFFORD WILLIAMS is also a graduate
of Wheaton College and Indiana
University where he earned his Ph.D.
He and his wife live in Deerfield,
Illinois. This is Williams' sixth book.